# Portrait
## *of a*
# Father

## HOW TO BE THE DAD
## YOUR CHILD NEEDS

# Portrait

## *of a*

# Father

## HOW TO BE THE DAD
## YOUR CHILD NEEDS

# CHIPINGRAM

Living on the Edge
© 2021 by Chip Ingram and Living on the Edge

www.livingontheedge.org

ISBN: 978-1-60593-409-9

# CONTENTS

# INTRODUCTION

I jumped into fatherhood early, with both feet and no experience. The day I got married, I became a dad.

I later adopted my wife's twin boys from her previous marriage, but at the beginning, I not only didn't know how to be a husband to their mom, but I didn't know how to be a father to them. And when we all moved to Texas so I could go to seminary, it got even more difficult.

Theresa and I were determined for her to be a full-time mom. I had to figure out a way to take a full load of courses while at the same time supporting my family. For four years, we were on a stressful and crazy but amazing and victorious journey. Our marriage got stretched, and God got bigger in our eyes. He came through.

At the end of those years, I had two eight-year-olds and a toddler. I had learned a lot, but I was emotionally out of gas, and I still had a thesis to write. I wasn't exactly eager to get the required research done, but I couldn't complete my graduate degree without it. I asked God what I should do.

I didn't hear an audible voice, but I sensed Him speaking. "Chip, write on the biggest needs you have in your life. That way you'll stay motivated." My biggest need? That wasn't hard to identify. I wrote my thesis on the role and responsibility of a father in transmitting values to the family.

I started by searching Scripture. I studied all the passages with the concept of "father" in them. I read a lot of psychological and sociological research to see what the world thought. I had piles of notes and lots of papers. But all I really wanted to know was the answer to two questions: *What's the role of a dad according to God?* and *What's his responsibility?*

## Who is a father supposed to be, and what is he supposed to do?

At the time, the general secular attitude toward fathers had been that they are important for genetic material but not much else. But three important contributions of fathers were beginning to emerge in the research: his role in moral development, his role in developing a child's sexual identity, and his role in a child's self-image. So I reviewed the literature, learned what the Bible said, and examined where the two lined up.

With three boys, this was not just an academic exercise for me. My own father loved me with all his heart, but his father had died when he was young, so Dad hadn't had a role model. He didn't know how to communicate love. Neither Theresa nor I had come from Christian families. And I wanted to raise my boys God's way. This was my pressing need.

I learned a lot in the process, and I want to share the fruits of my labor, with many more years of experience added in. Not surprisingly, it turns out that a father is extremely important. In fact, the health of a family depends primarily on having an effective father. After much more empirical research, the world now agrees: a good father is vital.

Yet nearly one out of four children will go to sleep tonight without one in the house.[1] That is tragic. The strongest predictor of whether a child grows up to live in poverty, become addicted to drugs, be imprisoned, or get pregnant or impregnate someone before marriage is to not have an engaged and active father at home.

The father is the primary shaper of a child's sense of right and wrong. He's the most significant influence on how a boy grows into his masculinity and how a girl understands her femininity and feels safe in it. Together with the mother, his influence shapes a

---

[1] US Census Bureau, cited in "The Father Crisis in America," National Fatherhood Initiative, https://www.fatherhood.org/father-absence-statistic, accessed March 16, 2021.

child's self-image. The mother has a strong nurturing bond with her children and may be more influential in their lives than any other person, but the still common idea that fathers don't matter very much is not at all true. The research says the opposite.

Knowing how vital fathers are is one thing; knowing how to be a good one is another. No matter how many fathers new dads have observed, we come into the role without any personal experience and little practical preparation.

**Knowing how vital fathers are is one thing; knowing how to be a good one is another.**

We hold that newborn—or, in my case, see two pairs of four-year-old eyes looking up at me— with many questions about the future. We are entering into an experience that can be challenging, stretching, and sometimes overwhelming.

Why is it so hard for men to be effective fathers? As I suggested, one reason is that many of us never had a good model. Some men can answer the question of what makes a great father by describing their own dad, but many can not.

Another reason is a shift in society. Today's culture has minimized the value and importance of fathers. It's increasingly common for women to choose to become mothers and raise children on their own. In popular-culture TV shows, fathers often play peripheral roles or are the butt of jokes.

I decided a long time ago that I would not look back at my children's lives and regret having only a peripheral role. I did not want them to know me primarily as a workaholic or a source of income. I wanted grown children who would look me in the eyes and say, "Dad, I know you weren't perfect, but I'm glad you were my dad."

That's what this book is about: raising children who will be able to answer the question of what a great father is like by pointing to their father's portrait.

We're going to look at four quick snapshots of a father in this book—the roles a biblical father takes on, according to God. I've organized these pictures using a simple format: a definition of each role, a key Bible passage that describes it, the questions someone in that role needs to ask, the focus of that role, how to walk it out practically, and the bottom line of what fathers are stewarding.

If fathers fulfill these four roles, their children's lives will be profoundly shaped for the better. I didn't do it perfectly. No one does. Expecting to meet an impossibly high standard will only cause frustration.

That's why I would like to walk through the following four roles with you, one dad to another. As you grow, you will give your children what God designed you to give, and they will be much better equipped to become who He designed them to be.

I hope you will find this portrait of a father to be helpful and inspiring and trust that your children will look back one day and be grateful that you were the dad they needed.

# 1

# Becoming
# THE LEADER
# They Need

One time I was at a coffee shop with other guys who regularly hung out to talk about being better dads. I was sharing my definition of the father's role as a leader. It covered everything: how he assumes authority and takes responsibility for protecting his family, providing for them, and helping them reach their full potential. It went on and on (that's just a summary), but I thought it was awesome.

The guys didn't. They looked at me like I was crazy. So I went back to the drawing board.

Now my definition of a leader is much shorter:
***A leader makes things happen.***

It's a definition a father can grab hold of. All
the elements about protecting, providing, and
mentoring are still important and true, but the
bottom line is that a leader does what it takes to
ensure that all those things are covered.

In your role as a father, that's your number one
responsibility. According to the Bible and the best
psychological research, you're *called* to be a leader.
You are the one who takes initiative in your family
to make the right things happen.

Paul used the metaphor of a father to describe his
relationship with the Corinthian church. Notice
how he describes the role of a leader in this passage:

> *I am writing this not to shame you but to warn*
> *you as my dear children. Even if you had ten*
> *thousand guardians in Christ, you do not have*
> *many fathers, for in Christ Jesus I became your*

*father through the gospel. Therefore I urge you to imitate me.* (1 Corinthians 4:14-16)

Do you see in those words the heart of a father who knows how to lead? These people had come to Christ and begun to grow spiritually, but they were hearing a lot of opinions from other voices about what they ought to do and believe. Paul wrote this letter to straighten out some problems, and this was one of them. He told these believers that they would have plenty of tutors, but he described himself as their spiritual dad. He wanted them to know he cared more than others.

Researchers have confirmed that modeling is the greatest way to socialize and educate children. It has more of an impact than anything else we do or say. But Paul wrote about this long before any research was done. He knew the power of example and told these believers to imitate him.

Jesus was the master of that approach. "Everyone who is fully trained will be like their teacher," He told His disciples (Luke 6:40).

Whether you like it or not, your children will grow up to think and act a lot like you. That may be scary, but it's also a great opportunity. If you want to have a positive, powerful impact on their lives, be the kind of person you want them to become.

## Be the kind of person you want them to become.

That doesn't mean you have to be perfect, of course. You aren't, and neither was Paul. He followed Christ with plenty of ups and downs, but he could still tell this church to follow Jesus in the same way.

And that's where making things happen begins. It isn't about getting your children to do what you want by being authoritarian. It's about shaping their lives by being an authentic follower of Jesus and showing them how to become one too.

## Questions Leaders Ask

Leaders are always asking three questions:

- *Where are we now?*
- *Where do we need to go?*
- *What must we do to get there?*

Sometimes those questions are subconscious, but they are still in the back of a leader's mind. If you've ever been assigned a project at work, you know this. These are necessary questions whether you're forming a team or launching a business. You don't approach major goals haphazardly and hope they work out okay. You don't do marketing without a strategy, build buildings without a blueprint, or spend money without a cost analysis and an expected outcome. Businesses and organizations assess where they are, think about where they need to go, and make plans to get there.

If you're going to lead your family well, you'll need to think through these questions at home, too.

I once said that to someone in the landscaping industry, and the lights came on for him. He realized how much focus and intensity he had at work, deciding how to irrigate and where to place plants, figuring out how the sun will hit them in different seasons, and analyzing all the environmental variables. Planning was second nature to him. He just hadn't applied it at home. So he immediately started figuring out how to plan for his family's success.

Have you ever thought about your family that way? Many men don't. We tend to let things happen and address situations as they come up. We may do some planning for major things like family finances, schooling for the children, and other similar logistics, but it's important to learn to think this way about developing our kids' character and faith. We have to focus on outcomes.

## The Focus of a Leader

The focus of a leader is ***objectives***. Is your family hitting the target? Are you headed toward the goal? Do you have the right goal in mind?

Have you thought about goals for each of your children? Not just that they will grow up to be solid citizens and committed believers with a decent job—that's all good but not very specific. At any given stage of your children's lives, do you have a specific target in mind for them?

> Your goal for your child, at whatever age, is to become more like Jesus.

At various seasons of their lives, I wrote on a three-by-five card one thing I was working on for each child. I kept it in my Bible, prayed over it, and reviewed it as I met with God. As a result, I naturally found myself rewarding, encouraging, and correcting toward that goal.

If you don't know what your target is, the world will figure it out for you, and you probably won't like the results. God gives us a really good target to aim for, and He promises to back it up. Your goal for your child, at whatever age, is to become more like Jesus.

God uses everything in our lives to move us toward that target. He uses our experiences, our parents, our siblings and our birth order, our struggles, our friends, our own idiosyncrasies, our dreams and desires, our challenges—everything.

That's the message of Romans 8:28-29: "God works for the good of those who love him, who have been called according to his purpose," because He has planned for us "to be conformed to the image of his Son."

That means that God is at work through everything in the life of your child. And you get to participate with Him in that process as the most significant human influence. But if influencing your child in his or her conformity to Christ isn't your target, you'll miss that opportunity.

Scripture actually uses targets as an illustration for raising kids. In Psalm 127:3-5, children are called blessings from the Lord, "like arrows in the hands of a warrior." They are a beautiful inheritance but one that needs to be aimed at something.

Have you ever seen anyone at an archery range shooting an arrow straight up into the air to see where it will come down? Or pulling back the string and letting it go with their eyes closed? Me neither. That's not how archery works.

Our children are like arrows, and we need to aim them. We want to put them in the bow of God's training program, pull back, and set them off in the direction of His calling.

Some of us have a lot of other targets mixed in: financial success, athletic prowess, academic accolades, popularity, a trouble-free life. Many of those goals are fine, so feel free to pray for them and thank God when they happen. But they are all secondary. It's possible to line kids up for success and watch them become successful failures if they haven't grown to become like Jesus.

We've all seen that happen—people who had everything going for them and achieved a lot of success but didn't have the character to carry it. That's not the inheritance we want to give our children. We want to give them the best.

## Next Steps to Take

This isn't always easy to do (anything worthwhile rarely is), but it is certainly doable. Both the Bible and research give us some practical ways to give our children the best and point them toward the target.

### *Model Christlikeness*

I mentioned modeling a few pages ago, and it will come up again. Role models are very powerful and very important. If your kids are going to turn out a lot like you, you will need to be a man of God's

Word, a man of integrity, and a man involved in healthy, loving relationships.

Again, will you do that perfectly? Of course not. If you read those words and decided you've failed already, think again. The point isn't for you to be perfect; it's to show that these things are important to you. Anyone can do that. If you are growing, your children will see that and will begin to grow too.

### Take Initiative

If you're a salesperson, you don't sit back and wait for customers to come ask if they can buy your product. If you're a journalist, you can't always wait for news stories to come to you. If you're in acquisitions, you're scanning for prospects, not just waiting for them to come ask if they can sign with you or sell to you. And if you're looking for a job, you'd better be out there looking for a job. One probably isn't going to just land in your lap.

If we know how to take initiative in other areas of life, we know how to take initiative at home. And the Bible tells us we should. Paul addressed fathers directly about this—not mothers or other family members, not the church or society, but fathers:

> *Do not exasperate your children; instead, bring them up in the training and instruction of the Lord.* (Ephesians 6:4)

There's nothing in that verse about hoping for things to turn out right. You take initiative and trust God with the outcome.

### *Give Direction*

Leaders also set direction—the target, the goal, the vision of Christlikeness. You recognize the unique needs of your children, how they are motivated, and what they relate to, and you leverage that to give them what they need spiritually, emotionally, physically, and relationally. You come up with a strategic plan, lay it out, and stick with whatever works while letting go of what doesn't.

For example, when our twin boys were in sixth grade, I realized I had neglected building their self-esteem through physical fitness. I knew how prevalent bullying could be in middle school. We started each day with push-ups and sit-ups, and they hated it the first few weeks. I did the exercises with them, and after a difficult beginning, they were excited as muscles appeared and they gained confidence. Soon they wanted to lift weights rather than watch TV, and it set the course for their teenage years.

### *Evaluate*

What happens when things don't work? You reevaluate. This is a constant part of the job, and it's a job that never really ends. What works at one stage of your children's lives may not work at another. Their needs change, so you look in the rearview mirror, notice where you've made progress and where you haven't, and adjust.

As I mentioned, I didn't know how to be a dad when our kids were young. My father was a good, moral man who cared for his children, but he had been through a lot, wasn't a Christian, and didn't have the tools he needed for raising children to become like Jesus. So I had to learn on the job, like everyone does. I can assure you that I did not get this down perfectly. In fact, I made a lot of mistakes along the way and, like all parents, have plenty of regrets.

**Nothing is as rewarding as having your kids tell you how much they appreciate what you've done for them.**

But God honors the desire and the effort to lead a family well. I now have a great relationship with my adult children, even though it wasn't always easy. You come up with a strategy, you butt heads, sometimes you feel like you've been through hell and back, and sometimes you confess your sin. But you hang in there, and it's worth it.

Nothing is as rewarding as having your kids tell you how much they appreciate what you've done for them or to get a card that says, "Dad, you've been the most powerful influence in my life." That's one of the highest goals you can reach.

That doesn't happen by doing things perfectly. You can give up that dream right now. I blew it often in ways I don't even want to remember. But kids don't need their fathers to be perfect. They need authenticity—the honesty and humility to say "I'm sorry."

That's modeling. Your children learn that they don't have to be perfect either, but they also learn that honesty and humility strengthen relationships. They become stronger followers of Jesus.

## Your Stewardship as a Leader

In a word, your leadership of your family is about stewardship. ***You are morally responsible before God for your home.***

Does that mean you take everything on yourself? Of course not. Just as you fulfill your own work responsibilities and allow others to do their jobs, you fulfill your responsibilities at home in the context of other family members. You own the moral responsibility; lead the way; take initiative to have a plan, a strategy, and a direction; reevaluate as needed; and go for it.

Sometimes when you start leading, it may feel awkward for a time, especially if your father didn't model it for you. You may also find that it changes the dynamics of your marriage. It can be a challenge at first—your wife may be a little uncomfortable with aspects of the new you—but it will be good in the long run. You aren't becoming a dictator; you're becoming a team. You come together and talk about the dream for your family and your children and how you both are going to work toward that goal. You partner with each other. But as a leader, it's on you to open that discussion.

I know this is a big job. You'll need help with it, so first ask the Holy Spirit to help you with your focus, intentionality, strategic thinking, and commitment. Then do whatever it takes to find some other dads who will join you on this journey. It's lonely when you lead. I always wanted to be learning from a father who was further along than I was.

Bring the commitment you show in other areas of life into your home. Bless your family with your humble, honest, but strong leadership. The rewards are awesome.

## 2

# Becoming
# THE PRIEST
# They Need

What comes to mind when you think of a priest? An elaborate robe or a black-and-white collar? A holy demeanor? An austere lifestyle? The image makes most people think of a special calling in a religious career—something that applies to a very small percentage of the population. If you're like most men, you think, *That's not me.*

But it *is* you. That's your calling—not the robe or collar or church responsibilities, but the dedicated life as someone who stands between God and human beings to facilitate that relationship. You are the head priest in your family.

And as a priest, your job is *to make God known*.

In Deuteronomy 6, we get a wonderful picture of what it means to be the family priest. Moses had presented the Ten Commandments to the Israelites. They hadn't gone all the way up the mountain as he had, but they saw the fire and smoke and heard God's voice, and it made them a little uncomfortable. So God essentially put Moses in the role of a priest: he would reveal God to the people and represent the people to God, presenting needs, hurts, fears, and petitions on their behalf.

So in his role as a priest, he begins to give the men instructions about being the priest in their homes:

> *These are the commands, decrees and laws the LORD your God directed me to teach you to observe in the land that you are crossing the Jordan to possess, so that you, your children and their children after them may fear the LORD your God as long as you live by keeping all his decrees and commands that I give you, and so that you may enjoy long life.*

*Hear, Israel, and be careful to obey so that it may go well with you and that you may increase greatly in a land flowing with milk and honey, just as the LORD, the God of your ancestors, promised you.* (Deuteronomy 6:1-3)

God wants His people to do the right thing, but that's not the primary focus of this passage. It's a means to the goal—that they would enjoy long life and that things would go well for them. He wants to bless them. He reminds them that this is a relationship—a promise He is giving them based on His character. A father's heart is about much more than following the rules. And that heart will show through in a priest's life and attitude.

> **A father's heart is about much more than following the rules.**

Through Moses, God is about to give His people a lot of content (the dos and don'ts for life in the Promised Land), but He also wants to communicate

His love. In the next few verses, He tells every father to instruct His children in the Word. They have to know it, but not in a rule-keeping, legalistic kind of way. His instructions are given to protect them from harm and allow them to experience the very best. He wants to put guardrails on the winding highway of life so His children don't fall off the cliff on either side. He has bigger, better, deeper, richer things for them than they could ever imagine.

So Moses, serving in the role of a priest, begins to tell Israel's men how to be priests in their homes. And he starts with the most important aspect, which is to make sure their family is worshipping the right God: "Hear, O Israel: The Lord our God, the Lord is one" (Deuteronomy 6:4).

### *To Impart Correct Theology*

The number one role as a priest is to impart ***correct theology***. I don't mean all the finer details and nuances that scholars debate and denominations divide over; I mean the core beliefs of our faith. In a world of competing beliefs, your children need to know who the real God is. They need an accurate biblical view.

### *To Cultivate Devotion*

Your next role as a priest is to ***cultivate devotion***: "Love the LORD your God with all your heart and with all your soul and with all your strength" (Deuteronomy 6:5). Don't just *believe in* the right God; *love* Him. Before any parenting you do, prioritize your relationship with God. Your children need to remember you not as a man of a certain vocation or certain hobbies, but first and foremost as a man who loves the Lord.

### *To Live a Word-Centered Life*

Then live ***a Word-centered life***: "These commandments that I give you today are to be on your hearts" (Deuteronomy 6:6). You can't know God apart from Scripture, at least not as fully as He wants you to know Him. You need to be saturated in His Word. It's actually a good thing for your kids to see you reading the Bible before catching up on sports or financial news. You want them to know you as a Word guy more than as a career guy or moneymaker or football fan. You can do any of those things, but they need to see your priorities.

They will need you to impart truth to them, and you can't do that if it isn't in you.

**Your parenting will come from who you are.**

I made a commitment to meet with God first each day—to read, pray, and ask for wisdom. Looking back, it was probably the most important thing I did for my children. It kept me centered, dependent, and sensitive to His will for me and them.

Have you noticed that the three aspects of being a priest that have come up in this passage so far are all about you? Your parenting will come from who you are, so pay attention to who you are. *Know*

*God, love Him with all your heart, and let His Word transform you.* Those are the most important steps you can take as a father and priest in your family.

But that's not where it ends. The Deuteronomy passage shifts from *being* to *doing*. As a priest, you are called to **teach**.

"Impress [these commandments] on your children. Talk about them when you sit at home and when you walk along the road, when you lie down and when you get up" (Deuteronomy 6:7). This teaching includes both formal training and informal conversations.

Israel's families didn't do a great job of this during the first few centuries, but by the time of Jesus, Jewish boys were learning the first five books of the Old Testament inside and out before they were twelve. And fathers were responsible. The synagogue helped, but it was the dad's job to put his children on the right track to understanding.

How do you do that in today's world? Start when your children are young with picture Bibles and books. As they get older, read them stories. Theresa and I did that with our children almost up to their teenage years, long after they knew how to read. We would read to them, and they would read to us.

Schedule times for teaching, too. The dinner table is a great place for that—not every night, necessarily, but ten or fifteen minutes a couple of times a week. Teach from the Bible and make it fun. Be creative. Ask questions, use visuals, and think of interesting illustrations and examples. Structure biblical reading and teaching into your family life—not rigidly or to a burdensome degree, but enough to keep God's Word in your minds and hearts.

But in addition to teaching your children formally, have conversations in the course of daily life— "when you sit at home and when you walk along the road, when you lie down and when you get up." Some of our best talks were while riding in the car. They would share about friends and crushes or about how their coach wasn't fair or their math teacher was too demanding. Those informal talks helped them handle those issues in their hearts and resolve problems in their circumstances and relationships.

God's Word is about life. It's relevant to everything. You don't want to be known as someone who has only a Bible verse for every situation, but you do want to offer wisdom and shape perspectives with God's truth. Let your

> **If the Word is woven into your heart and mind, it will come out as needs arise.**

conversations go there. If the Word is woven into your heart and mind, it will come out as needs arise.

Then **practice it**. Apply the Word to every area of life. "Tie them as symbols on your hands and bind them on your foreheads. Write them on the doorframes of your houses and on your gates" (Deuteronomy 6:8-9). That may seem like an odd instruction in a modern context, but it essentially means to integrate God's Word into your doing (hands) and thinking (foreheads), your activities, your work, the things you look at, the hobbies you enjoy, your church life and community life—*everything*. You walk it out.

Some of our most holy times were lying on the concrete after playing basketball, sharing our deepest desires, and praying out loud together as father and child. More than a few major crises in our family were addressed by an emergency family time-out, we all sat on the floor in the living room, joined hands, and prayed. Sometimes the crisis was that we needed money to pay rent; other times it was that a family friend was in ICU at the hospital. More than anything, I wanted our kids to know that God is not just for church on weekends; He is our life.

Having laid out the roles of a man who is a priest for his family, Deuteronomy gives some amazing promises. God will take His people into the Promised Land and give them great cities, houses, vineyards, and olive trees, and they will eat well and have satisfying lives (Deuteronomy 6:10-11).

Those are specific Old Testament promises, but they reflect God's heart for His people. He may bless you spiritually, relationally, materially, or all of the above. But when you live His way and honor His Word and pass your understanding and devotion to your children, He will certainly bless.

Your children will visit homes and see families where this is not happening, and you want them to notice the difference. They need to see the benefit of a home where a dad is caring and engaged and committed to God and His Word. They need to see your affection for your wife when you think they aren't looking. They need the experience of a father who has a joyful and fulfilled heart.

You'll go through hardships, and you'll have down times, when you aren't at your best. That's okay. You may never have a lot of money, and sometimes you'll get sick, but that doesn't mean God isn't blessing you.

But if you keep bringing Him into your struggles and theirs, He'll keep coming through in ways that are meaningful to you and your family.

Your kids will remember that. They will learn how God works. As much as I hate to admit it, the times of challenge, disappointment, and suffering we experienced as a family were formative and powerful for our children.

When life is going well, it's very important not to start focusing on the gifts instead of the Giver. That's the message of the next verse (Deuteronomy 6:12). And it's important to maintain your focus as a priest by worshipping and serving God alone (Deuteronomy 6:13). Your character, convictions, integrity, loyalty, dependence, and entire life are all centered on Him. He is to be the focus of your thoughts, feelings, actions, words, and lifestyle. You can enjoy everything He gives you to enjoy, but He remains the centerpiece of your life.

# Questions Priests Ask

How do you get there? Just as a leader is constantly thinking about questions of direction, a priest is always thinking about questions of devotion:

- ***Do my kids know God?***
- ***Do they have an accurate view of God?***
- ***Does our home honor God?***
- ***Are we growing in holiness?***

First, ***Do my kids know God?***
The ultimate purpose for every human being is to know and love God. This is His goal for them, and as a priest in your family, it's your goal too.

Second, ***Do they have an accurate view of God?***
Your kids are being bombarded all the time with different views of God, from whether He even exists to all kinds of distortions about His nature. In the midst of all those voices, you need to intentionally present an accurate understanding of who God is.

Third, ***Does our home honor God?***
If Jesus walked into your house, sat down on
the couch, and observed your interactions, your
attitudes, your values, the way you deal with
conflict, the things you watch on your TV or
laptop, and all the other aspects of your home
life, would He say, "Well done," and tell you He's
comfortable living with you? Or would He say, "I
think we need to talk about some of this"? Would
He see that He's being honored?

If you're living out a double standard, telling your
kids one thing about God but not showing that you
believe what you say, it isn't going to work. Children
can accept our failure and imperfection, but they will
not tolerate our hypocrisy. Your kids will do what
you *do* more than they will do what you *say*.

Finally, ***Are we growing in holiness?***
Holiness is not the same as always carrying a Bible
and being strict, somber, and no fun. It means
being winsome, free, pure, and set apart to God.
It involves moral purity in our thoughts, words,

and actions. People who are holy are different from the world around them—not weird, but distinct. Teenagers who enjoy being with their parents, siblings who know how to resolve conflict, couples who have been married twenty-five years and still have a spark—these kinds of things stand out as positively different.

That doesn't mean everyone in the family always gets along or that there's no friction when your teenage kids are appropriately developing their own identities apart from their parents. But as a family, you should be growing in ways that demonstrate the holiness, love, and goodness of God. Living out His ways at home should create an environment of love, joy, and freedom. And that's different.

## The Focus of a Priest

All this can be summed up in the word *worship*. That's your focus as a priest. Everything you say, think, and do as a father should be rooted in worship. Don't think of worship as only singing songs in church services; I'm talking about living every day to honor and glorify God in all you do (Romans 12:1). That's what the instruction in Deuteronomy 6 was centered on, and it's the reason behind those four questions we just looked at. It's at the heart of your ministry to your family.

That might sound intimidating. In fact, this whole chapter may seem like an overwhelming journey. If that's the impression you're getting, relax.

The journey is an essential part of the assignment, and wherever you are on that road, it's okay. You have everything you need to move forward with God's help.

When I wrote my thesis about what a father is supposed to be, I looked in the mirror and realized I didn't fit the picture. I was overwhelmed, and I told God so. I figured my thesis would be good enough for my degree, but I didn't know if my fathering would be good enough for my family. Thankfully, I sensed the Holy Spirit's voice: "Chip, would you lighten up?"

God is a patient Father. He gets excited when we take baby steps in the right direction. If you have children who have learned to walk, you can probably remember how much you cheered them on when they took their first step. You didn't say, "Just one step? Come on. Get with the program. Run!"

God doesn't say that to you, either. Take a step toward Him and He'll start leading. Step by step, you'll get there. You'll look

## God is a patient Father.

back in a year or two and be amazed at where you've been, and you'll be really glad you took that first step. Finding some men to share the journey with you is critical for success. You cannot go wrong by guarding worship in your home and serving your family as a priest.

## Next Steps to Take

Practically, what does it look like to take steps in being a priest to your family?

## *Model Authentic Worship*

It begins again with modeling. What you demonstrate is important. That can involve certain activities—going to church, being in a small group, listening to worshipful music or sermons—but you aren't going to be significantly transformed unless you're regularly getting into God's Word. Remember what God told the Israelites? The first instruction after loving Him with everything in you is to let His Word be on your heart (Deuteronomy 6:6). That has to be a priority for you as a dad.

Don't let yourself believe the idea that you don't have time. Everyone has the same amount of time. How we use it is a matter of priorities. If you need to get up fifteen minutes earlier, do that. Read thoughtfully and prayerfully every day. If you don't know where to start, begin with the gospel of Mark or John or the book of Acts. Just start.

Then pray for your wife and each of your children each day. Pray for the people you will meet with or work with that day. If you do that daily for a year, your wife will have a different husband and your kids will have a different dad. You'll have peace and rest in your heart and probably a better attitude toward home, work, and most other things.

### *Initiate Family Worship*

Priests don't wait for others to initiate worship. They don't have other people drag them out of bed to get ready for church. They set the direction and prioritize the things that God wants to happen.

Your children may tell you they don't want to go to church. That's fine. They don't have to want to. Just tell them you love them so much that you are going to take them anyway. It won't scar them for life or destroy your relationship with them. One day they will respect you for it.

Don't make church your only worship experience for the week. Initiate family worship time too. You don't have to have family devotions every night; in fact, it's best not to because you'll either burn out or miss a few and feel like the whole effort failed. Set one night a week and stick to it as often as you can. The devotions don't have to be fancy or take very long, and there are plenty of resources to help. Just get into the Bible a little, talk about it for ten or fifteen minutes, and pray together.

### Encourage Private Worship

Your kids will need to develop worship practices of their own: some prayer or Bible reading before bedtime when they're young and in the morning as they get older. Try turning off the TV or limiting screen time a half hour before bedtime. No TV show, video game, or website is likely to change their lives, but God's Word will. Have them spend a little time each day reading a book that will encourage them spiritually or praying for their friends.

These practices can go a lot deeper as they get older. Introduce them to some great Christian authors who will make them think. Check in from time to time. "What are you reading? What do you think about that? What is God teaching you? How can I pray for you about that?" It can lead to great conversations.

## Just do life together and learn together.

In my kids' high school years, I unashamedly paid them to read some books that I knew would be foundational to their development. You can pick out some books for you and your kids to read and have some great discussions about them. Don't make it legalistic; if they miss a few days, tell them God understands and encourage them to get back into it.

None of this has to be complicated. You don't have to be an expert on the Bible or be well read in Christian literature. Just do life together and learn together. It will establish lifelong habits that your kids will not regret.

## Your Stewardship as a Priest

Your stewardship in this area is ***to own the spiritual climate of your home***. In most American homes, the woman takes the lead in establishing that environment. And most women would love for their husbands to take this and run with it. It won't be easy; anything of value will take focus, energy, strategy, discipline, and intentionally. But it will be one of the best decisions you've ever made.

Ask God to help you with that. He's the perfect Father; He knows how to walk with you, encourage you, and give you wisdom and strength. He will always show you what the next step is. And in any setback—you'll have some of those—He will give you insight and ideas for trying something new. He will help you become a better dad as you create an atmosphere of worship and lead your family in faith.

3

# Becoming
# THE TEACHER
# They Need

Imagine yourself in a traditional high school or college classroom of your era. Do you remember how it used to be set up back in the day? Rows of desks or tables, with the teacher up front doing his or her best to impart information.

Depending on the teacher's effectiveness, you may have learned a lot, been thoroughly bored, or something in between. In most classes, lectures were supplemented with readings, and you were tested on everything you had learned. Over time, you were exposed to different ideas and branches of knowledge, most of which you've probably forgotten. Everyone does. You can retain only so much in this model of learning.

Now get that picture out of your mind as you read this chapter. Teaching isn't opening up our kids' heads and pouring in a bunch of information, hoping it will be retrieved the moment they need it. No, that's not the biblical model of education. In the Bible, ***a teacher imparts wisdom and builds character***.

That's your role as a teacher: imparting wisdom and building character. Another term for it is to make disciples. It's about applying knowledge to life, developing a lifestyle characterized by wisdom and understanding. It doesn't come simply from information; it's a process of training.

The book of Proverbs defines wisdom for us and then shows us how it applies. Wisdom is understanding how life is created and how it works best in our relationships, words, attitudes, and actions. Not only do we learn what to do, but we come to understand the why behind it all, develop discernment about when and how to put knowledge into action, and then pass that wisdom on to our children. They learn God's patterns for life, enjoy the protection of good decisions, and experience His *shalom*: the fullness, wholeness, completeness, and blessing of His kingdom.

As a teacher, your job is to build values, convictions, and principles into your children's lives. You don't want your kids to just learn a few skills; you want them to

> **Your job is to build values, convictions, and principles into your children's lives.**

have character—to be faithful and full of integrity in every area of their lives. Then when they get into their transitional years and are making decisions on their own, they won't just follow their peer group; they will pursue what God wants because of how He has worked in their lives over the years.

Proverbs puts a lot of emphasis on fathers giving wisdom to their children, but this is a New Testament theme too. A verse we looked at earlier expresses it clearly: "Fathers, do not exasperate your children; instead, bring them up in the training and instruction of the Lord" (Ephesians 6:4). Did you notice who this verse is addressed to? *Fathers.* Mothers, Sunday school teachers, youth group leaders, and plenty of other people can help, but the responsibility is primarily on fathers.

This verse says not to exasperate your children, frustrating them with unreasonable burdens or causing them to get angry. That's the negative half of the command, and I've unfortunately experienced what happens when I ignored it. I exasperated my children by being perfectionistic and having expectations that were beyond their level of maturity. That's a fault-finding approach, and all it does is produce anger. I've also been too passive at times, been too harsh at times, and made my kids not want to listen to me or embrace my values. Being a good teacher means steering clear of those extremes.

Paul follows the negative command with a positive one, and it's all about training. Instead of being too harsh, too passive, too perfectionistic, or too anything, bring children up in the training and instruction of the Lord. The word here for "bring up" is very broad; in classical Greek it meant nourishment of any kind. The way Paul uses it here gives us a comprehensive picture of nurturing and developing the whole person.

It also gives us a two-pronged approach: *training* and *instruction*. Some translations use words like *discipline* and *admonition*. The first word implies actions; the second implies words. And the order of these two approaches is important.

When your kids are young, they can't follow detailed instructions or even understand why you're giving them, but they do respond to consequences: small rewards and punishments given lovingly and kindly to reinforce what you're teaching them. Early on, by way of your actions, you lay down the railroad tracks of life. Then your children know what's right and wrong, what you expect of them, and how much you love them.

Then, as they grow, you use words to keep them on course. If you've laid down those railroad tracks well, you can avoid many instances that most parents have experienced: talking, explaining, arguing, then yelling to get your kids to do what they're supposed to do. Your words will carry weight because you've long demonstrated that they are consequential. Your overall goal is to bring up your children in an atmosphere of godliness in which you educate, impart wisdom, and build character by your actions and words.

## Questions Teachers Ask

Teachers approach their roles with a set of questions, just as leaders and priests do, and sometimes the responsibilities of teachers will overlap with those of leaders and priests. To be an effective teacher in your family, you'll need to keep these things in mind:

- ***What do my children need to know, do, and be?***
- ***How do my children best learn?***
- ***When and how will I teach them in this season of their lives?***

First, ***What do my children need to know, do, and be?*** The way I envision that question helps me remember every part of it. I think about the need to develop their heads, their hands, and their hearts. They need certain kinds of knowledge and specific life skills in order to become the people God has called them to be. That's true in their character, motives, relationships, career paths, work ethic, finances, decision making, and devotional lives. It's comprehensive.

That's why it's so important to move past the image of a teacher as a classroom instructor. In parenting, you haven't done your job just by giving your kids the right knowledge. There's much more to it than that. The goal is not for them to know a lot but to have transformed lives—to put knowledge into practice in real-life situations.

Second, *How do my children best learn?* If you have more than one, you know that whatever worked well with the first one may not work as well with the second. Two of my children were born within five minutes of each other and grew up in the same family environment, but they learn completely differently. They also responded to correction differently. One was compliant after just a stern look, and the other still wasn't compliant no matter how many intense arguments we had or how many times I grounded him. You'll need to learn what's best for each of your children based on their personalities and ways of communicating.

Third, *When and how will I teach them in this season of their lives?* Not only is each child different, but so is each stage of life. When our kids were small, Theresa and I read Bible storybooks to them. Because she spent so much time with them during the day, evenings would often be my time with them. We'd shut the door, pile up the pillows, get close, and make it fun. I wanted them to hear the content of God's Word with that warm and secure association: cuddled up with their dad's arm around them.

That approach obviously doesn't work in the middle-school years. Instead of at bedtime, we did it around meals because I wanted them to have their own time with God before bed. Once or twice a week around the dinner table, we read the Bible and talked about it for a little while. I tried a million approaches, and some of them worked for about three weeks but then stopped working and would have to be adjusted again. The kids were growing and changing.

Now that they're adults, I'll send them a link to a message or give them a book. Sometimes they'll even say, "I'm ready for a good book, Dad. Give me something to fire me up." When they visit, we'll talk about what they've been reading or listening to, and

I'll find out what God's teaching them. It's a loving, nurturing environment for sharing the ups and downs of our spiritual journeys with each other.

The point is that every season is unique, and you'll need to figure out how to communicate God's Word, both formally and informally, in a way that gets it into their hearts and lives.

## The Focus of a Teacher

A teacher's focus is *wisdom*. We want to help our children apply knowledge and understanding from God's Word in every area of their lives. Fortunately, there's a section of the Bible devoted to that purpose. We call it "wisdom literature." Makes sense, doesn't it? It includes Job, Psalms, Proverbs, and Ecclesiastes, and if you want to train your kids in important life skills, these are great books to start with. Take them through the book of Proverbs chapter by chapter, verse by verse. It covers issues like character, relationships, sex, work, finances, the power of words, and much more. The Psalms show how God's people have responded to painful circumstances and great victories with raw emotion, prayer, worship, and celebration. Pray them out loud together.

When your kids get into the teenage years, use the book of Proverbs to talk about sex, money, and friends. Work your way through Ecclesiastes with them. At a time of life when they are figuring out their identities, they will need to know that life won't be satisfying if it's rooted in money, pleasure, education, status, popularity, or anything else except God and the purposes of His kingdom. Solomon—the wisest, richest, most powerful man in the world—came to that conclusion after trying everything. Without God, everything is "utterly meaningless" (Ecclesiastes 1:2). It's a great lesson to get early in life.

Over time, lessons from these books will do much more than fill your children with knowledge; they will give them a solid biblical worldview.

## Next Steps to Take

Much of what we talked about for the role of a family priest also applies to the role of a family teacher. Here are two practical things you can do to effectively teach your children.

### *Model a Word-centered life.*

You probably guessed this was coming. Modeling is the first step in every role you have. And living a Word-centered life is central in every role too; we saw that in the previous chapter because it came up in God's instructions in Deuteronomy 6. You will get the wisdom your children need from you by saturating yourself in the revealed truth of Scripture.

### *Provide formal* and *informal instruction.*

I fell into a common trap years ago by thinking that because my kids went to school, it was the school's responsibility to educate them. And that's true, to a point. Children will learn to read, write, and verbally communicate in a variety of subjects at school. But that doesn't mean those skills will be fully developed or that they will get all the education they need there.

When I noticed one of my children getting good grades but not thinking and communicating at the right level for his age, I had a soul-searching moment. I didn't want to stand before God one day and ask why the school hadn't done a better job with my son. His teachers accomplished a lot, but the responsibility was on me to prepare him for the future, so I decided to do something about it.

I pointed out to him that he wasn't doing much work and was still getting good grades, and I expressed my concern. I told him, "If they aren't giving you a challenge, I will." So we started going through a book on major themes in the Bible. I had him read a section, look up all the relevant verses, and answer the questions in the book. Then we talked about what he had learned.

He got into that. We went through most of that book, and eventually he was writing papers for me. I'd tell him what he had done well and where he needed a little more work, and he learned a lot. We did the same with a C. S. Lewis book, and my son outlined every chapter and identified the flow of thought in each. He started using that logic on his teachers, and it turned into quite an advantage in his favor.

> Your stewardship as a teacher is to transfer godly wisdom to the next generation.

Eventually, I had him give mini-sermons on what he had learned. Theresa and I sat on the couch in the living room and listened. He got pretty good. He soon developed a love for theology, learned how to write, and discovered how to articulate his thoughts. His confidence grew, he did even better in school, and best of all he developed a love for learning.

You don't have to take that same approach, but you do need to be creative. Work truth into your children's lives formally and informally. Notice teachable moments—failures or challenging situations that open their hearts to advice. Don't focus on what they've done wrong; help them explore what they can do right next time. Remember the goal: you have an opportunity to impart truth to your children that will make you and them very grateful years later.

## Your Stewardship as a Teacher

Your stewardship as a teacher is *to transfer godly wisdom to the next generation*. You'll have your own way of doing that because you know your own strengths and what works best with the personalities in your family. But it will take some discipline and persistence. Training is a lifelong process.

Theresa and I made a decision early on not to have video games in our house or let our children have

TVs in their rooms. And on school nights, none of us would watch TV. Those rules may not work in every family, and I'm not saying they ought to be everyone's goal, but we felt that this was important for our family. We noticed that media-centered homes were very often not Word-centered homes, even if Christians were living in them. We wanted to be different.

My kids didn't like that very much. Sometimes they got bored. But getting bored creates great learning opportunities. Sometimes they would grab a guitar or play the piano, lift weights, or shoot hoops in the driveway. Sometimes they would pick up a book and start reading. Amazing things happened. They learned to think and be creative. Today, all four are voracious readers, musicians, initiators, and communicators.

Again, I'm not saying those policies are a template to follow, but I offer them in case they are helpful. You will have to decide what's best for your family. But whatever you do, make it your priority to teach—to provide information, impart wisdom and understanding, train behavior, and coach your children in life situations. Or, as Paul put it, to discipline and admonish, to bring them up in the training and instruction of the Lord.

## 4

# Becoming the
# LOVING DAD
# They Need

Juan grew up in Mexico with seven brothers and sisters. His father lived in the United States and returned home briefly about once every six months. During those visits, his father went out every night, got drunk, and came home to beat his family. He never showed his kids any love or affection.

Juan later found out that his dad had another wife and three daughters in the US. When that wife left him, he brought the girls to Mexico so Juan's mother could raise them along with her seven kids. Juan told his mother often that he would never be like his father.

But Juan got married when he was eighteen, mainly to get out of the house, and the marriage ended after a year—but not before a son was born. Juan abandoned the boy, just as his father had abandoned him. A few years later, he married again but often beat his wife out of jealousy. Another son came out of that marriage, and after six months, Juan abandoned that family too.

Several years later, Juan got married for a third time—this time to a Christian woman. He fell into the same pattern. He beat his wife, and he also beat his second son and shunned the first. After nearly going to jail, he tried to be a good father, but his efforts never got him very far. He made promises but never kept them. He tried buying his son's love by giving him clothes and toys. But he never gave him what he needed most: his time. He did exactly what his father had done to him.

Juan eventually became a Christian and felt led to mend fences with his first wife and son. When he talked with them, his son asked Juan where he had been during all the holidays and birthdays—where he had been when the son was in jail for stealing to prove to a gang that he was a man. What was so wrong with the son that his father didn't want to have anything to do with him? Crying, his son told him that he used to wait by the phone on his birthdays, hoping Juan would call—just like Juan had when he was a boy. He just needed to hear his father say he loved him.

Juan started attending our church, and God began to change his life. Over time, he let go of his anger toward his father and reconciled with him. They cried and hugged, and Juan finally heard his father say "I love you." He also began growing into a good role model for his sons. He told them he loved them. He was finally learning how to be a father. And when his sons graduated from high school, he was there.

Fathers are called to love. Someone who loves ***gives people what they need most***. That's what God has modeled for us, even at great sacrifice. He's an unconditional lover of our soul.

What do people need most? It usually comes down to *provision* and *protection*. Those are comprehensive words—not just material provision and protection, but spiritual, emotional, relational, intellectual, and moral. A father looks with love at his children and thinks, *Whatever they need.* Maybe it's a tender hug or a firm consequence for their behavior. Maybe it's giving a little encouragement or meeting a big need. Whatever it takes, you care for them. You literally give them your life.

> What do people need most? It usually comes down to *provision* and *protection*.

The last two verses of the Old Testament are about restoring the relationship between fathers and their children:

> *I will send the prophet Elijah to you before that great and dreadful day of the LORD comes. He will turn the hearts of the parents to their children,*

*and the hearts of the children to their parents;*
*or else I will come and strike the land with total*
*destruction.* (Malachi 4:5-6)

Jesus tells us that the Elijah figure mentioned here is John the Baptist, who came to prepare the way of the Lord. One of the effects of the Fall is ruptured family relationships, and one of the signs of people living under the kingdom of God is a heart-to-heart connection between fathers and their children.

Jesus paid attention to children. In that era (and in many others, too), kids were ignored by adults and were thought of as needing a lot of attention without contributing anything. When parents brought their children to Jesus for prayer and blessings, the disciples stopped them. But Jesus rebuked that and said, "The kingdom of heaven belongs to such as these" (Matthew 19:14).

The more secular we become, the more society pushes children to the margins. They are often portrayed as burdens, inconveniences, drains on finances, or hindrances to careers. There's nothing wrong with family planning, but the motivation shouldn't be about kids cramping a person's lifestyle. In the kingdom of God, they are priceless.

## Questions Loving Dads Ask

If you're focused on giving your children what they need most, you will constantly be considering three questions:

- *How are my kids really doing?*
- *Do they sense my approval and acceptance?*
- *Are we connecting at a deep level?*

First, *How are my kids really doing?*
Some people don't pay much attention to their car as long as it's running. Others check under the hood periodically to see how things are going. That's the kind of father you need to be: check under your children's hood to see what's happening—not just what their report card says or how well they're doing in their games or performances, but what's going on inside.

How are they handling moods and challenges and responsibilities? What motivates them? Who are they hanging out with? Notice any emotional withdrawal or stress and explore what's really happening.

Second, ***Do they sense my approval and acceptance?*** Your kids need to know that you are *for* them. You want to bless them because you are on their side. It's not enough for you to feel approving and accepting of them; they need to know it.

> **Your kids need to know that you are *for* them.**

I picked up some important lessons from a friend of mine. I'd see him grab his son, give him a pat on the shoulder, and horse around with him. He'd give his little girl a hug. When his kids were within earshot, he'd say things like, "They are the delight of my life." He was their cheerleader.

I realized from him how much we need to communicate with both words and touch that we love our children. They will face plenty of rejection in their world, and they need to sense approval and acceptance at home. That's a huge part of love.

Third, *Are we connecting at a deep level?* When kids aren't happy with you, they tend to withdraw. When you probe to see why, they deflect by arguing. It may be that everybody else's parents will let them do whatever they want to do—I've heard it many times at almost every age—and your children are greatly offended that you don't. But if you sidestep the argument and dig a little deeper, you may find out important feelings that are behind the desires and motives.

Many parents respond to a child's withdrawal or resistance by withdrawing too or by dismissing it as "teenage years" or "just a phase." If you're concerned about the kids they're hanging out with or the attitudes they've adopted, be courageous and give them some clear boundaries out of love. Make time to connect, even if they don't want to. I've had to say, "You and I are going to have breakfast together once a week. I'll sit quietly and listen, or we can just stare at each other. But I'm your dad, I love you, and we're going to be connected whether you like it or not."

They may *not* like it for a while. But eventually they'll love you for it.

## The Focus of a Loving Dad

As a father motivated by love, your focus is ***relationships***. That can be really difficult if your father didn't model healthy relationships as you were growing up. Like Juan's, your natural trajectory will probably follow the example you were given as a child. But you don't have to follow the same path.

You can learn how to love the way God loves. Again, take baby steps and let Him give you wisdom and strength every day. He is on your side, just as you are on your children's side. He is fathering you, as you are fathering them. I've seen many men completely shift their focus, rearrange their priorities, and learn to express love clearly and sacrificially over time. You can do it too.

## Next Steps to Take

To be a leader, a priest, a teacher, and a loving father in your home, you'll need to take some specific practical steps. And, as always, the first one is about living it out yourself.

### *Model loving relationships.*

Modeling a love for God and for your wife is one of the healthiest things you can do for your children. Watch your attitudes and your words. Treat your mate the way God treats you. You've blown it, and God has been gracious with you, so when the people in your house blow it, be gracious with them. Things aren't going to be wonderful all the time, but when you maintain your love even when other people are making it difficult, you are demonstrating God's heart.

This applies even when your mate is no longer in the house, by the way. If you're divorced, be very careful about what comes out of your mouth. I've seen it happen again and again: parents who bad-mouth the other usually find their words backfiring when the kids get older. It's poison, and it doesn't reflect God's grace.

Be intentional about modeling His love for you in your relationship with others, even if there's bad history there. Your kids will be emotionally healthier for it. And when you fail to do so (and you will), just own it and tell them that you're sorry you blew it and that's not who you want to be. I cannot tell you how many times my wife and kids have heard me say that. Surprisingly, now that they are adults, it's what they remember most—not that I had it all together, but that I humbled myself and owned it.

### *Make time.*

There is no substitute for time. Your kids want you to be there. And when you're there, you need to be *all* there—not just physically, but also mentally and emotionally. Quantity *and* quality are important. Your family understands you have other responsibilities and interests; you don't have to give them all up. But you do need to prioritize, and your schedule has to reflect those priorities.

***Provide tender love unconditionally.***

God gives us a great picture of Himself in Psalm 103:13: "As a father has compassion on his children, so the LORD has compassion on those who fear him." When a father is loving well, he is compassionate, tender, caring, and approachable.

What does that look like? First, you can be tender with words. If saying "I love you" isn't easy for you, force yourself to do it and get used to it. Tell them before they go out the door. End your phone conversations with it. They need to hear it. Everyone does.

Tenderness goes beyond words. Touch your children, as my friend I mentioned earlier did with his kids. Give them a hug; put your hand on their shoulder; wrestle with them when they're little. They need to be connected to someone strong, and wrestling is a safe way to give them that sense of security. As your daughters enter their preteen years, the dynamics of touching change, but don't back away. They need the comfort of being touched and loved nonsexually by a man who cares. Your daughter will choose a safe, good man if she has learned that there are safe, good men. Be that for her.

You can express tenderness in special moments, too. Celebrate their awards, graduations, games, performances, and other accomplishments. Make birthdays big—not necessarily expensive or with lots of people, but make it clear that they are a big deal to you. You're celebrating a really important event in your lives.

When they get hurt—their first breakup, their disappointments, their losses—they especially need your compassion. Don't lecture. Just listen to their hearts and hurt with them. When they have big decisions, make it a point to listen more than you give advice. If you listen well, they will come to you for advice later and be much more open to it because they initiated the conversation.

## Deal with the behavior later, if you need to, but show your love and acceptance first.

And finally, be tender when they fail. They will make choices you don't like. That's part of learning. Deal with the behavior later, if you need to, but show your love and acceptance first.

I told my kids, "There is nothing you can ever do that will cause me to stop loving you. No matter how badly you blow it, I will still love you. You can always come to me; there may be some

consequences, but I will always be there for you."
Years later, one of my sons, during his formative
years, got sucked into pornography and was
devastated. He told me later, broken and crying,
"I knew I could tell you, because I remember
hearing over and over that you would never stop
loving me, no matter what." In every situation,
lead with love and address issues afterward.

### *Provide tough love when necessary.*

Your kids are always asking two questions: *Do you
love me?* and *Can I have my own way?* The answer to
the first one is always yes. The answer to the second
is often no. Tough love makes those answers clear.

Here's why:

> *No discipline seems pleasant at the time, but
> painful. Later on, however, it produces a harvest
> of righteousness and peace for those who have been
> trained by it.* (Hebrews 12:11)

There will be times when you have to lay down the law and enforce consequences when it is broken. But don't make it just about enforcement. Let your kids know that love is always the reason for your boundaries. Tell them that you love them so much that you won't allow their attitudes or actions because it isn't good for them.

You can calmly say things like this: "I know it's a bummer, but when you do that, you can't use the car." "Whether you can go to the party or not is up to you; here are the conditions." "When you neglect your responsibilities, here's what happens." "You can make it as hard or easy on yourself as you want, but this is the deal." And then stick with it.

One of my sons had a rebellious attitude for nearly four years, and it was making our family miserable. We eventually had to have a really hard conversation.

I reminded him that we loved him and that nothing would change that. But I also said, "Although we don't have a lot of rules here, we do have some boundaries. You need to have the right attitude and behavior, and if you can't do that, it's time for you to find somewhere else to live."

Don't ever have that conversation unless you are clearly led by God or know there's no alternative. It's incredibly painful, but that's where we were.

Our son hibernated in his room for a few days. Then he walked out and started living like the person I knew four years earlier. After a few more days, I realized he wasn't just putting on a show to manipulate. I asked him what changed.

"I just wanted to know where the boundaries were."

My jaw dropped. We'd been through four very tough years—for boundaries?

"Dad, I've heard about God all my life. I know it's true. And I know you and Mom really love me. But part of me wanted to go off and do my own thing, even though I knew it was wrong. You wouldn't let me, and that made me really mad. I stuffed it inside and kept pushing to see how far you'd go. I found out. I know rebelling against God and you isn't worth it. I'll live my life the way I'm supposed to. I had a good talk with God about it."

> Always give your kids what they need, but don't always give them what they want.

I changed more in those four years than at any other time in my life because I needed God like never before. Looking back, I realized that I did well with boundaries but failed to really understand the struggles in my son's heart. Thankfully, he not only set a new course with Christ but also forgave me for my part in that difficult journey. That son grew up to write Christian music and preach the gospel through song, and today he's grateful for not getting to have his own way.

One of my professors, the late Howard Hendricks, used to ask, "Do you want your kids to love you next week, or do you want them to love you ten years from now?" When you don't provide boundaries because you fear your kids' reactions or you cave in and don't stick with consequences you spelled out, they learn that you aren't serious, and you'll lose their respect. Always give your kids what they need, but don't always give them what they want.

## Your Stewardship as a Loving Dad

Your stewardship as a loving dad is ***matters of the heart***. The leader stewards a moral responsibility, the priest guards the spiritual climate, and the teacher imparts wisdom and builds character. The loving father watches over the heart of the family.

If your kids are older and you're thinking it's too late to be the father you were meant to be, stop. It's never too late. Go back and read the story that opened this chapter for the evidence of that.

Your adult kids still need you. God has a way of making up for past mistakes in light of today's obedience. He can restore the years the locusts have eaten (Joel 2:25). He can give you returns on a recent investment as though you had invested years ago. Pour out your life and your love into your children regardless of how old they are and see what God does.

# CONCLUSION

I want to encourage you to learn and apply four specific principles that will help you become the dad your kids need you to be.

### 1. It must begin with your thinking.

Don't just hope these snapshots stick; let them sink into your heart and mind. Read this book again and again if necessary. Because I didn't come from a Christian home, a lot of this was foreign to me. But even if you're familiar with these principles, knowledge isn't enough. These truths need to become part of you. That's the only way they'll show up in daily life.

## 2. It only becomes real with support.

Don't try being a dad on your own. Find a group of men to talk to. Learn from other couples. Connect with people who will keep you accountable, brainstorm ideas, and share successes. These don't have to be formal arrangements. Just find some people who are struggling with parenting too and work at it together.

## 3. It requires supernatural grace.

You'll need grace to model what we've talked about. If you've never asked Jesus into your heart to forgive you, cleanse you, and empower you with His Spirit, do that today—first because you need it, but also because your children need it from you. You can't put this book into practice or learn from your mistakes without the supernatural grace of God.

## 4. It is sustainable by pondering the future.

I picture myself in my late seventies or early eighties. I lean back in my chair, envisioning my birthday and everyone who is gathered there, and I think about what will really be important then. It won't be the size of my house, how much money I have, the kind of car I drive, or how many members my church had. It will be the people who are there: my kids and grandkids. Will I be able to look back and see that my legacy was raising children who walk with God? Will you?

That question and that vision keep me going through all the challenges that come with being a father. They will keep you going too.

# BIBLE STUDIES by
# CHIP INGRAM

## Available at LivingontheEdge.org

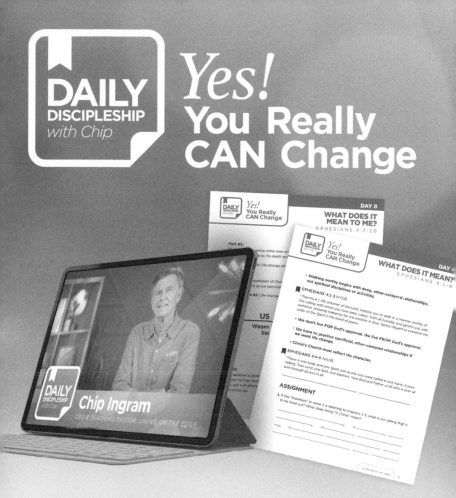

## HAVE YOU GIVEN UP ON CHANGING?

Join Chip Ingram for Daily Discipleship. This free 19 day video study, with downloadable study guide, will show you that yes, you really can change!

Available at:
**LivingontheEdge.org**

LivingontheEdge.org